RE

WAITING FOR THE

Roger Moulson

Waiting for the Night-Rowers

821 MOU

ENITHARMON PRESS

First published in 2006
by the Enitharmon Press
26B Caversham Road
London NW5 2DU

www.enitharmon.co.uk

Distributed in the UK by
Central Books
99 Wallis Road
London E9 5LN

Distributed in the USA and Canada
by Dufour Editions Inc.
PO Box 7, Chester Springs
PA 19425, USA

ISBN 1 904634 26 5

Enitharmon Press gratefully acknowledges the financial support of
Arts Council England, London.

British Library Cataloguing-in-Publication Data.
A catalogue record for this book is available
from the British Library.

Typeset in Bembo by Servis Filmsetting Ltd
and printed in England by
Antony Rowe Ltd

ACKNOWLEDGEMENTS

Thanks to the editors of *Magma*, *Poetry London Newsletter*, *Poetry Monthly*, *Rialto*, *Stand*, *The North* and *Tying the Song* (Enitharmon Press, 2000) in which some of these poems first appeared.

Thanks also to my teachers Michael Donaghy, Jane Duran, Mimi Khalvati and my mentor Elaine Feinstein, and to Jane Duran, Mimi Khalvati and my editor Stephen Stuart-Smith for their comments on the manuscript, to the Thursday groups for their companionship and to the staff of St Mary's Hospital Paddington for enabling me to finish this book.

For Jackie

CONTENTS

THE WOODEN PIANO

Its makers wanted most to learn to hear, and chose
to learn by building it, shaping each piece by hand.
Two things were difficult, but no one said,
hiding anxieties under leaf and branch.
For hammers, jarrah wood. Tock tock, gung gung.
They only spoke at evening as the piercing blue
flooded the mallee and black peppermint.
For string, they said, the stringybark in our backyard
will do. They twined it, waxed it, pulled it tight.
Straight after morning it was always evening.

Ironbark rang, and still the blue was creeping in
through dusty leaves for they had not invented felt.
They said, We'll make the keys from scribbly gum.
If it were evening all our lives, said one with ears,
we'd never finish. A candelabra
was too complicated, they all agreed, and
unnecessary. The rest was easy, pedals
smooth to touch. When it was finished, they waited
for the longest evening of the year to flow
through tuarts, woollybutts and flooded gums.

The one with ears played klung klung tlock tlock,
a melody her fingers found. Oh, play some more,
they cried, and turn your ears to find that sweetness
in the wood we worked. She played. She swayed. They lay
and listened as she pedalled and felt sounds
plucking at their bones. If we had evenings every day
as long as this, they said, we'd learn to hear so well
we'd spend our lives in listening and say, This
is our work. How it must hurt to really hear.
Klung klung, she played, plink plink, kaloom kaloom.

STOCKS

Sea-worn timber, close grain, lean years,
rings standing above the times of plenty. I had time
to gather it, I had time you understand.
And most of those stocks and limbs of wood,
they were lying there. Lying there some of them,
or rolling up the beach and down again and drifting off.
Some had to be rescued. To be rescued
and stuck in a basket. And for what? To be the evidence
of something you've done? Rescued, but they didn't need
rescuing, no, didn't need resuscitating
like the taxi driver who was swimming oddly,
then rolled on the sand and we couldn't resuscitate.
The lumps of trees and stanchions had been long dead.
But not rotten, all their stuff scrubbed and salted down,
cellulose maintaining its integrity like bone,
fibre knocked to roundedness, drawn
and stringy, fine and pale, the way you get
as you get older. One I rescued from a cave jugged out
with stones, glugging, cold as the Greek hell.
Yes, I had the time to do it.
And like all you save – if you've saved anything
you know – it turns right round, wants to roll over you,
roll you right down the shelving beach and back
into the surf and you have to give it away
for some other fool to possess. You still have time,
the same as me. Remember how old Odysseus woke
on the sand not knowing he was home, not recognising it,
the beach like any beach. Bits of wood wearing
to the silver of things long in the sea, slipping
from the words we hold them by
towards some new category, the unrecognised
– *What is it, Dad?* – unrecognisable, matter
scarcely breaking surface, yes floating, but only just.
Next thing we come to are the stones.

TURNING OVER

The ground is easier than I thought. It's dark
and clingy, not the yellow clay I feared.
Twigs, roots, weeds to compost. I leave old bones
thrown for some dog long dead and guess how human
fossils will be collected like ammonites
by some new species. I expose what's hidden.
No treasure, unless you count a brass drawer handle,
a biro top, a piece of an old clay pipe.

The blade clangs on pebbles left by a glacier
till my hands are as polished as the handle.
I know there's something here I haven't owned.
I leave worms and wireworms, kill larvae, slugs
and snails. Their lives are unimaginable.
They work their darknesses in muscular purpose,
sentenced for something they haven't done.
A robin watches, avid for live meat.

The earth smells of winter. I struggle with roots
of trees. They are not twisted except to pass
what's too hard to go through. I follow them
into the clay where they reach straight and clean.
They are the candelabra the green world
holds to the dead. When I cut them it is severing
what lies here, a friendship, a hard won comfort.
They resist, break, and the frayed ends reproach.

A FIELD OF STONES

The rain has cleaned us,
says a broken stone,
and soon a frost will pencil in our edges.
Our labouring in the dark to heave ourselves
from bedrock, to get thrown up.
It seems so long ago.
We call ourselves the land's surf.
Who, if they really see us, does not love us a little?

Not all have eyes, a flat stone says.
I heard a tractor driver say
You sit there like birds along the furrows.
What are you waiting for?

Who ever heard of a stone aching?
Any that say so cannot be true stones.
Some believe in a final landfall, a land of basalt.
We believe in becoming more like ourselves.

We don't want to fly like birds,
says the flat stone, All that flapping.

We want to fly without any weight.
It only needs one of us to do it.
Just think, if all the stones suddenly lifted up,
people would say, The land is sinking.
The land is leaving the stones in a field of air.

The flat one says, They'd say the stones
want to fly into our mouths and kill us.
The stones want to wear coats of blood.

Or it might be night
so our flight darkens the stars.
We'd make patterns no one else would see.
Next morning they would look at the field
and say That field used to be covered with stones.
The farmer has cleared them
and the earth looks better.

WAITING FOR THE NIGHT-ROWERS

Word is the rowers start and square their blades.
The hills attend. They're crazy for release,
for night to find its marker pen and cross
them out with clear firm strokes in parallel
so they can cool and breathe and be forgotten.

The view's an array of pockets lined with pinks
and saturated greens filling with shadows
of velveteen. A mist is rumour of their breath,
rehearsal of stroke, cheating the ears of those
that dread the silent dipping of the blades.

Windows reflect the skyline and pass the torch
to factories moulding matter into things,
lulled with repeated motions, easy desires
for sex and cigarettes, flick, flicker, gone
in drawing in and slow express of air.

A steel flue tapers like some endless waist
cooling what passes in and out, solids
turning into smoke that's dark by day and pale
by night. Now to be breathed, down the long strain
of ribs, is wanting's blue turned indigo.

Lungs work to reach the end of all their lines
till every throat goes dry and soughs like wind,
for nothing runs the length of violet
and if it did no voice would stretch that far
except the rowers' song, too low to hear.

Now moons illuminate the inlets and fumes
stream brownly over stone as evening pushes
bodies into doorways. Light gentles around
largenesses, leaves some of itself behind
against the stare of faces bending to the water.

Pulling its slugs of oxygen cold wind
feeds fire through the channels, flame without light.
Lovers use lamps to measure emptiness.
Hungry for cold fetchings, fixings, gettings,
they brave the approaching silence of the blades.

They seek the usual intensest colours
and ask Will it be soon? and practise standing
very still to imagine the force and calm of love.
They empty themselves entirely, prepared
to be displaced, to bear the passage of the rowers.

Things that had been thrown among wet leaves,
bags of broken brick over the axle,
plywood opening its lamina
like a book, a squeegee mop
as nibbled as a toadstool, its rust-handle
floating islands of chrome,
stacks of plastic pots curving like palm trees,
a roll of roofing felt
and cardboard home to blood-red worms.

Borrowing their gravity
I take the corners slow so they won't hardly move.
There's green gravel in the voice of the roofing felt.
'I've never been unrolled.
I hold myself so tight, you know.
They told me I'd watch the clouds
while I did some good in the world.
I wanted to see the sea. What is it like?'

I'm wondering how I can describe the sea,
its animality, variable skin, its shrilling of surf,
when in the mirror I see the pot-columns sway towards me,
and speak in turn.
'First the darkness.'
'Then the house of manufacture.'
'Then the house of sale.'
'Then the house where we were to be given a purpose.'
'The house where we might be in the presence of love.'
Here they bend down between singing and sighing.
'Then the being put to one side.'
'Being thrown in the wet leaves.'
'The journey from the house of love.'

I feel the car low on its suspension,
open the back and hug the roofing felt
up the steel stairs. I wrestle it to the rim
and it unrolls into the waste.

THE GLASS OF WATER

Amazed to find the thing it most desires
light strikes.
Glass rings around it.
The contents accept their shape
but do not own it
as if shape's the need to be held.
Water does not concern itself
which one holds
and which is held.
The glass stands on the ghost of itself.
It shines a beam through shadow
speaks of volume
of a single column.
Water waits to run.
It breaths into the mouth of air.
When it's most still
it is compelled towards the other always.

BETH ORTON'S VOICE

Like a black kite in an updraft, like a burger box lifting
its square cups like a bra flying high up a high rise,

like a stricken spire with a ball at its tip, like a top or a tap root
reaching in air, fixing on upwards, like fuliginous smoke

catching, cutting light on the page of a book, catching fire
like a worn cotton print tearing softly, parting thread

after thread, like a choice of channels and none of them works
and the one that does isn't the one and then it is, then it is

and you get I'm on the . . . I'm on . . . and she says . . . if you
    like . . .
like an exchange you hear through a wall that has you

wondering, waiting to hear the next act, awakening anger
or hunger . . . like it was there in the room all along, a beseeching,

intractable pulling, bitterness you drink from a glass that others
have drunk from and you need them to say yes, yes it is.

FOR A LOAF IN THE BLACK OVEN

For the bright flowers of the field and the field itself
at the day's end I am waiting for your salt and scorch
and for the strong heart of fear that fills the centre of the table
as I wait to hear the mills making small the achievements of my
    days
so I can rub their meal between my fingers.

On your own you are enough, broken and breathed,
a love that is out of love, drinking the sweat of my palms,
returning the dirt of my fingers to generate new lust
from that part of me consumed, burned in each particle of black,
so that, light failing, I have that patience to eat your proving from
    the cloth.

TREE BAGS

Bare winter boughs holding thin tattered bags,
a plague blown from a row of shops.
It is their emptiness that calls to me,
the way they fill with wind,
fly and collapse, snagged like shreds of moon
struggling to free themselves
    as they are being torn,
flapping at me like flirts
or roadside grass waving each passing car.

They touch my emptiness,
all the rags I've hunted after as if they know a way
inside of things where surface
is reversed and shaken out so meaning's gone,
weightless and pierced, coverings
desperate for bodies to impress them. Skins
    that once contained
must learn how to be held to view, shone through,
forms without content, washed in and out of.

No content? One holds an inch of rain
and like a heavy fruit pulls down a branch.
Juice that's no juice at all. The rest
are shells and what emerged from them who knows?
Wind gifts I call them, bubbles of separate thoughts
like good intentions worn so thin the good's
    a ghost of nothing.
Here are the wrappings of too many things
not love. Bring me no gifts that I can use.

WATER LEVELS

Quick. Catch me if you can. I am myself
and you'll find nothing purer in your life.
I'm always clean, not dirtied by the burden
I carry to the sewer. You want me to

but I won't play at mirrors and hold still
conspiring with you in your careful pose.
No one's that beautiful. I wrinkle over
and give you back yourself entire and trembling.

I am more true to you than you are to yourself.
I shake before you know you're shaking.
Why else do you stare at your shivering image,
or there on the bridge turn from me screaming?

I'm transparent in covering up my depths
revealing yours. What is it you see there?
What you once were and what you might become?
Well, here I am. Let me kiss you all over.

THE STEPPING STONES

There weren't any.
Across my path a river came from nowhere
out of the bogs of Rannoch,
black sinews, muscles, back so sleek
that nothing broke the surface.
No boulder could lift its head with her on its neck.

I reached beneath her for a rock,
its face worn smooth, turned to her constancy.
I felt her moving in my arms
and slowly learned to move with her.
If I couldn't say the right thing I said the wrong thing
into the dizzy waters of her dress,
the deep cut of it,
the fretted reach she dragged across the broken floor,
the polished slabs of that drowned ballroom.

She was cold to touch
as if she'd danced so long her heat had cooled
to some extreme of need.
I was going to say she was all over me
but she would have been the same with anyone.
I heard her beating,
my ear to her dark breast.
I thought she said, *Step carefully*
but not too carefully.
Lean into me waist to waist.
Her hair smelled peaty, newly washed,
poured through my fingers.
I knew we'd met somewhere before
and knew we'd meet again.
She said, *Keep talking, move your hips.*

I told her how well she moved, things I won't repeat,
things I never thought before.
I whispered what she hadn't known she wanted
and then I slipped or she rose up
gripping me so cold I felt her heat,
and all at once she loosened, fell away.

In her wide arms I danced from bank to bank.
Under water the stones I stepped on.

FIELD GUIDE TO THE BIRDS OF BRITAIN AND EUROPE

The male great northern diver swims
motionless in summer plumage
beside its double dressed for winter
on the same wave. *On breeding waters
gives loud screams and yodels.* And then
Maniacal laughter. Plate 1.

The albatross is steering clear
of mariners and such. The crow's
not doing anything disgusting.
While doves are listening for the obvious
rhyme, the grounded lark keeps stumm,
and swans are all reduced to scale.

There's a king but no queenfisher,
a night but not a dayingale,
many sparrows, one sparrowhawk
three different bustards, one sole shag,
and a display of tits, mostly male,
blue, bearded, marsh, coal, crested, great.

They all share the same piece of sky.
The red and black kites, the hen, marsh
and Montagu's harriers, the booted
eagle, the honey and common
buzzards fly up the page in perfect
formation, each with its markings.

Five hundred birds in full colour.
They fly auspiciously from right
to left. Or sit in puddles stuck
to their reflections. Or perch on twigs
detached from trees. Or, standing rapt,
feet grip the white of paperspace.

OOVV

Who needs words to think
or feel? I load their cargo.

If they have wings, so does
any noise. The eyes of an owl

dragging a broken foot
over snow. It looks O O

it hops V
       V.

If it could take off and land
it would winter in the barn.

THE BELL-BIRD

I'd like to hear the bell-bird sing
Its keyholes in the air
I'd like to hear the bell-bird's song
Unlock what's hidden there

I'd like to hear the bell-bird's song
Then cut it with a knife
To make a second wedding ring
And give it to my wife

I'd like to hear the bell-bird sing
Softly to all our children
Until they feel its song take wing
Out of the power within them

I'd like to hear the bell-bird sing
So I can touch each note
To thread their colours on a string
Around my darling's throat

I'd like to hear the bell-bird's song
Filling a jug with water
So when the pitch grows high and strong
I'll pour it for my daughter

I'd like to hear the bell-bird sing
Until the woods resound
With furious strength to break and bring
The dead out of the ground

I'd like to hear the bell-bird sing
And touch an old friend's sleeve
I'd like to hear the bell-bird's song
Before it's time to leave

BY THE RIVER GADE

A storm is forecast, a dark absence, something unsatisfied
bending towards this sky with its burden of rain.
A mother collecting conkers with her child
looks warily at this stranger walking through the wood
towards the mown grass of an English park.

There! Dense blue, grey chevrons, flying above the water,
neck doubled, a heron

lands by a stream below Jebel Gumbiri,
black and white monkeys crash through branches,
and baboons drill me with yellow eyes, smelling my flesh
and calculating. By the rest-house the caretaker sits,
smokes her long pipe, checks the fire
and taps sticks spoke-wise under the pot.
Leonardo shows me the lulu tree, tells me how soldiers
looted the fittings and shot the ghazal and elephant
for meat, for money, for the joy of it, to prove themselves men —
and the war goes on. In five months the lulu tree
will fruit, women collect its small pulp,
fire consume the head-high grass
and in burnt ground crocuses will flower,
the time of burning being both a winter and a spring,

and I see the wary mother and think of William Lukudu's child
strangled while selling cakes.

AT ARKANJELO'S

Jubek has come. He is the fifth to sit down.
Will you take something, says Arkanjelo.
Jubek pulls a ball of cassava from the cassava bowl,
dimples it with his thumb, dips it in the gravy bowl
and eats. He eats fast. *What news?* asks Sebit.

There was fighting at the well, says Jubek.
The guest girl, Rita, was filling her bucket.
Kenyi was there. He said, Fill my cup.
She refused. He overturned her bucket.
She insulted him. He beat her with his fists.

Five hands pull the last of the cassava.
Augustino fills the jug. We hold out our hands.
He pours water over them. From hands it runs
to the ground. Drops bounce and ball in the dust
which won't receive them, a dull soft sound.
No one wants to talk about the fighting at the well.

THE LAND CALLED LOST

A heaven of umbrellas floats across
the land called Lost. Its fields are ankle deep
in hankies, socks and tights, knickers in a heap,
the shine of rings and earrings, precious dross.
The air is thick with swirling scarves that toss
a multitude of single gloves. These keep
on looking for their pair and never sleep
while spectacles like moths alight on moss.
Lakes fill with sighs condensed to rain, with sand
from tired eyes, while clouds grow dark with fear
and touch the ground to search the rocky slope.
I've looked but you're not here. You're in the land
of Gone-for-good where all the paths fall sheer.
No whisper, not a breath of you, no hope.

BY THE HALOGEN LAMP

I have never been in a room where everything is still.
When I asked my blood to sleep in its pipes,
it refused, politely but firmly pushing through the valves.
Rooms are the same. They never listen.
Their thick walled silences are rude and sullen.
I wish they'd shut themselves up.
One day I'll come straight back in
and catch them practising to be blocks of something solid.
Yes, music can do it,
threading me on its string of notes, opening my mouth
and sending me into the night to catch flies.
Simple kindness.
Eyes too, those that have held me in a space
where I can feel the elegance of mathematics,
where I can change the terms.
A parabola has me smiling.
So show me the night sky held in your eyes.
If you can't, never mind,
I'll imagine it for both of us.
Would you like a sine curve or a logarithmic?
There. Do you feel it? Pure daftness.
Or shall we sit, me here, you in a room
in whose window a different night shines,
and imagine we are both watching
the dust in my lamp's light?
Or, since it is a law that no room is stilled,
I will imagine the street lights streaming in your window
while you imagine the motes in my beam
brilliant with you.
Doors haven't been invented yet.

WE WALK ON SNOWY HILLS

The mountain's flank's a phrase I've often read
but never heard. Beware – it's the kind
of day one might forget and use such words.
Say something joyful's in my mind

to ask of Sarah, knowing she'll give me
that tidal look of grey floods meeting
in her eyes, then do it, finding those words
that really are, a form of greeting

by which we know ourselves. And yet I'm silent.
Crust on the snow and we take turns
in front, making boot-deep prints – one side
is dark, the other almost burns –

and the print-maker's shadow goes far out
across the slope. I hear her voice
though she hasn't spoken. The left is bright,
blackness on the right. Which? The choice

matters, but less than the treading of it.
Ice fastens as the light is ebbing.
We watch the sun gleam once and then it's night.
Sarah's prints are too small to step in

but there's comfort in following the line
and length she takes – and so I sound
the set and rhythm of her walk. We go
by the faint shining of the ground.

COUNTING

Maureen in marketing had eyes so dark
I couldn't tell you what colour
they were except wells you shouldn't lean over
but somehow couldn't help.
She did sales forecasts for this year,
next year, the year after that, every year till the end
of the world. She made sense of crazy numbers,
numbers I didn't even know were numbers,
exponential curves, best fits,
what-if scenarios.
She keyed the number pad with a small frown
and went into a trance, fingers
fluttering over the Toshiba
so fast she got the machine in a logic loop
so the display twinkled
with twelve digit numbers
endlessly digesting themselves.
When I had to query some of her figures
she was fierce in her defence of them
like they were her children and she loved them all
down to the third decimal place.
We couldn't agree,
and we couldn't agree.
Then she smiled me a smile and said
What we gonna do, Roger?

NOTHING

for Georges Ifrah

The dot on her forehead increases her beauty tenfold
just as a nothing dot increases a number tenfold,
writes Biharilal, and I think of Andrea Saxton
with the dot on the palm of her hand she's drawn in black pen
and shows to the girls and the boys she likes. Hundreds, tens,
units, borrow one, take away, pay it back. We put them in
columns and it's right or it's wrong and nearly right's
wrong. Mrs Rowlands is smart but she's always polite
when you make a mistake. Russell Hibbert says to Julia Cupitt
'What's a unit?' and she says 'You are, you nit,'
and Andrea looks with her smiley brown eyes.
I secretly love her but nobody knows.
The stars had begun to shine in the sky like marks
for nothing as if they had been in the fine blue-dark
of Brahma's skin and he summed them all up as he taught
with a piece of the moon which glowed in his hand as chalk,
says Subhanda. Andrea's finished her sums, draws noughts
on one finger and shows me her single black dot.
It's nothing, yet so powerful I stare. 'You can touch it,'
she says, 'if you want.' On her arm she has freckles, like dust is
so close you can't count all the bits, the millions and billions . . .
Mrs Rowlands didn't say, didn't know the Indians
made the nine numbers and nothing, 1 body and skin,
2 ankles, 3 worlds, 4 positions, 5 arrows, 6 limbs,
the horses are 7, 8 serpents, the body's 9 holes
and *Shunya*, the Absence, the Void, and finally told
Khalif al-Mansur, and when the Crusaders returned
from Jerusalem they brought the new numbers they'd learned,
nine arabic signs and the empty place, *sifr*, then
gave them to a Europe still figuring, struggling with IVXCDM,
and then Mrs Rowlands gave them to us.

Julia says 'I got ten out of ten. What did you get, Russell? My sister says boys have only got one thing. She says girls have got two.' 'I got eight.' 'That's nothing,' she says.

HORBURY

The name might be Saxon for the pasture by the marsh, I forget
and I'm not checking because it would only mean sheep grazing,
swine marsh or something. That's the Saxon colonist.

All I remember is the visitor saying, It has to mean the place
the whores come from. She was right of course,
and with the whores the pimps and loan sharks, tax accountants,

roofers, riggers, couriers, bailiffs, tax inspectors, and that's not all
but it's enough, each with a piece of Horbury in their pocket
they bring to London, to anywhere that's not a pasture by a marsh,

anywhere that has a different smell, of money say, juice bars or
    ozone
drifting off computer banks. You see the Horburys wash through
    streets
shown in the A-Zs, only their having left the place in common,

their escape from a language too intimate and not intimate enough.
Horbury's the stone in the shoe, the mispronunciation of a word
you read but never heard, the wrong measure, the discomfort

of knowing its whereness, its special hooks, the lover that might be
waiting somewhere, the long look from a stranger you catch
reading their wish and yours to find the Horbury in each other.

You see them in pubs. No? Well, let's have a drink. We recognise
each other now. You mesh your fingers. I'll play translator of
    tattoos.
You think your knuckles say f u c k o f f, but I read h o r b u r y.

It seems so far from here, like when you look for stars and the city's
   glow
is too bright to see what's there, what happened in that room
light years away in Horbury. Hard to focus – I'll have the same
   again –

and not flood the world with private pain like the child from
   Austria
displacing half of Europe, but find the impersonal place each
   Horbury holds
in the universe, its gravity growing immense the smaller it gets,

seen only by the light you surround it with, its unreturning of
   sheep
that stray into the pasture by the marsh. Let's keep this watchful
   calm.
Let's drink. Call Horbury what you like but call it by its name.

ROWING GRANDMA

Your pointy hips were the oarlocks
and your hollow tummy seated two.
We said *Row, Grandma, Row,* and you beat
your arms and raised dust from the carpet.
We said *Row* and your nose pointed true
north and our boat shook with the speed.

As you washed at the sink we saw
your back, a clinker on the sand
at Bridlington, all ribs and keel.
And later, much later, before
you died, you became a shell, a hand
held against the light, a lemon peel.

We said *Make waves*, and then you raised
your skirted knees like sails and pushed
with your feet to jiggle us back
and forwards, or, feet apart, rocked
us from side to side, till we lurched
to the floor from your slidey frock.

When we came in, you turned the radio
off, the waves that kept you afloat.
Grandpa brought you from that far place
to live with his blunt people and made you
happy sad because you found them cold.
In photos yours was the smiley face.

We said *Make a storm, Make a big
sea,* and you pushed hard with your legs
and jerked your tummy off the ground
and bounced and nearly made us sick
till you threw us up to your chest
and held us both there, safe and sound.

After Grandpa died and beached you
among strangers and graves, for two years
we rowed you till we grew too heavy
for your tummy and tired you out
ride after ride crying *Make waves make waves*
and then *Make a big sea, Grandma.*

TO SWIM WITH OPEN FINGERS

That lump of water was a shock to see,
how it shook its see-through skin
and swelled between its tiles.
Then someone shouted and it took
that noise and threw it back so loud
and wrong I shrank, as if the light it held,
through shock, had turned to sound.

At school we went to swimming lessons.
We shallow-enders whooped and hollered,
pretended we were raising hell
and when another joined the swimmers
whooped louder for we felt more lonely.
I loved them all because I knew they could
have had their mothers write them notes.

I loved them more when I became
a swimmer, when my hands made paddles
and learned to pull above across
a depth I didn't want to think about
unless I looked, unless I stopped and asked
what happens if I fall. Only not stopping
kept me suspended over deeps.

Today I swim with open fingers.
Making along dense lines of turbulence
I am becoming something webbed
in this constant cool embrace.
It has one dream, its dream of flood.
See how the fish slip through my fingers.
I reach for what I cannot see or touch.

MY UNDERSTANDING OF SHOE LEATHER

My grandfather liked to polish his shoes
after he came to stay. They were so black
I saw the ceiling lights in toecaps left
and right and, flitting round them, I caught shadows
of family. I saw my head but not my face,
two huge noses and ears four to the pair.

Of mirror opposites they formed a pair.
He used to clean my grandma's high-laced shoes
before she abandoned them and turned her face
to the wall. If she was a swan, she was a black
one, not mute but deaf. I guess suspicion shadows
her still, as angry lonely as when she left.

I know he always started with the left
out of courtesy to her, then did its pair
and when he'd finished, lifted the glossy shadows
to the light as though he were seeing not shoes
but her in that long Edwardian dress all black
but for the silver brooch and solemn face.

Waxing insteps, seams, tongues, he bent his face
to work as if mending a thread they'd left
broken in the mill and rubbed his thumb end black
in the welt, the same thumb he used to pare
tobacco from a plug as dark as his shoes
then tamp it in the bowl and light the shadows.

He liked to sit in a room of dancing shadows,
bake himself, spit in the fire and seek a face
from his union days, the lads all smart in shoes
and jackets, their politics leaning to a left
still bright and new, when they ran away the pair
of them and got married, when his hair was black.

He cleaned my shoes once, made the scuffmarks black.
Then someone said I should be ashamed. The shadows
of growing up, doing for myself. The pair
of us stood for a moment face to face,
then crossed over till he lay down and left.
I took the brush he used and cleaned my shoes.

In shoes' black shine his disillusioned face.
I brush the shadows deeper since he left,
his hands in mine, two pairs to polish shoes.

THORNWICK

Small caravans – tin eggs – pale cream, deep cream,
beige, colours I imagine, across the field
tilting towards what will become blue sky,
holiday blue, where dad stops work midstream
baffled, where grass ends and the bone hard wold
drops to a shore. It's almost dawn. The sun hides

on the sea's far edge and I see the high up air
changing to purple, but here the night holds on.
The clutch of caravans is cold with dew
on towels left on lines and folding chairs.
I watch them find their proper colours, renew
the paint on faded panels, turn trims golden,

see handmade curtains in misted windows, pegs
like squiffy soldiers in a line, bucket
and spade, the red blade gathering redness out
of nothing so I see each thing made fresh
and new and want to run between and hug them
one by one. The sun climbs with a sudden shout

over the cliff herding a thousand shadows
and in a flash they stripe the hills, then furl
back to the things they're tied to. My head
on a blue door flies to me like a sudden sorrow
and I wonder why the sun makes live things dead
and who's in the blue caravan. It might be a girl.

A curtain moves. It is a girl. I run
to the cove and put my cheek against the chalk,
smooth and round. I taste the salt. By the water
a crust of limpets, winkles. Rim of brown.
Plush red anemones plump the rocks. In cracks
green ones wave purple tips, languid pointers

that say 'This is the sea. The rules are different.'
Weed channels shine with chalk, the submerged limbs
of bodies waiting till the moon says 'White rock!
Which stones will leave their deeps and climb the cliff front
to see a starlit land where shadows swim?'
and then they'll rise, shake off the sea and look.

I listen to the pebbles seethe and chatter.
'Neither here nor there. Between. The sea so cold,
the land so hard.' A foot slips on the kelp.
The girl. 'Why are you talking to yourself?'
'I'm not.' 'I heard you say, "The sea so cold,
the land so hard," like that. So sad like that.'

HALF THE POOL WAS LIT AND HALF IN SHADOW

Half the pool was lit and half in shadow
Because the sun came slanting through the glass

And chose to touch some heads and leave the others.
Half the pool was shadowed by the half lit up.

Some heads so caught the light they dazzled others
And caps of swimmers moved from dull to red,

From grey to white. The way sun raked the water
It was a harrowing of arms and shoulders,

A deep enjoying of what broke the surface.
Half the pool was lit with cobalt water

And swimmers swam towards its burning blue
Wanting their whites white, their reds red.

Out of shadow faces came to brightness
Washed of sorrow, their shadows under them.

A STAR FOR MRS STRINGER

What would you be wanting with a bit of lead?
If you find me a piece I'll make you a star.
I wish you would lad, Mrs Stringer laughed
and reappeared with ends of pipe and flashing.

I made my mould of a piece of wood I carved,
a five-pointed star,
bent the flashing to fit in the crucible
my uncle brought from the black lead works,
put the glossiest coals on the fire, opened the grate
and pulled the damper out till it fairly roared.
I held the crucible over the heat with tongs,
bent over it till I was burning, held it
at arm's length, changed hands, the hot metal smell.

When the crucible turned cherry red,
the flashing melted round the edge,
slid into itself, dross floating on the brilliance.
It poured so easy, water from a jug,
and never dripped or spilt, went right down,
looked for the bottom of the mould and settled.
The wood took its heat, smoked, caught fire
and I tipped it on the hearth. It didn't clang.
Its lustre oxidised to grey
like people you see clear first time you meet
but after clouded by what's passed between.
This was the first star.
The second larger where the mould was burnt.

I took the second for my sheriff's badge.
Its points were Law, Justice, Courage, Understanding, Peace.
The finer one, the first, I gave to Mrs Stringer.
It was still warm.

Put me a hole in it to hang, she said.
Bright spirals curled around the gimlet
as I cut it through, then threaded it with string.
She held it to her lips then bit it.
I said It's poisonous to put it in your mouth,
and told her the five names I'd given.
You think you know a lot, lad, but you don't know nowt.
She put it round her neck.
The star slipped out of sight, hung heavy.
Her breasts rose like silver fish, dived,
and swallowed it.
She shivered and took the five points.

THE ORNAMENT OF MY AUNT

I live on the East coast, she said, I live by the sea.
She was my favourite aunt although she wasn't my aunt.
I liked the way she walked across the room
and then sat down like water collecting in a pool.
On my first visit she left me alone with my wishing
she were my real aunt.
Out of the window far off beyond pebbles and marshes
I could see the real sea.
But I was alone with the porcelain wave on the table,
its green ropes of brine always breaking
between smile and wait for a kiss.

On top of the frozen wave, a boat. In the boat a man.
She called him Dusty because, she said, he always was.
His rod had no line, but he stared
at the spot on the table where the line would have entered
as if a fish would jump out of the wood.
We know he won't catch a fish, she said,
because the fish is too slippery for the likes of him.
He doesn't know but we know, don't we? she said.

Only I knew his wanting to could pull a mermaid
from the oak. Once I heard a shrill cry
and imagined his arms dragging her into the boat.
There were six silver scales on the table.
I didn't tell my aunt who wasn't my aunt because . . .
because . . . the sea was calm and the mermaid beneath,
hopelessly white, long hair in the grain.
I polished the table top to look for her.

My aunt Who-was-not came to stay.
She said, The first wave was black with pebbles
and shattered the French windows.
The second was green with glass
and broke in the middle of the room and took possession.
She said, I was standing in my black ball dress in the sea
and my friend never came.
Now you'll have to protect me.
I still feel the glass in my legs and it hurts when I sit.
I'll never live by the sea again, she said, never,
and gave me six sequins she'd saved from her dress.
I went in the bathroom, stuck them on my skin.
I said, I live on the East coast, I live by the sea.

REX RENDEZVOUS

Tomorrow this place will be a library.
Before it was a parking lot.
Before it was the Rex Rendezvous Ballroom.
I stand at the vanished door.
Its slat of light illuminates my shoes.

We went to get real rock and roll, me, Col and Dave.
Our tutor said we'd better start with something simple
like the waltz, and showed us one two three.
Her smile was imperturbable.
There were twenty-three people, older, taller, women.

We envied Dave his five foot nothing.
He breathed the air of cleavages.
My first partner had a bosom,
floured, vanilla scented, like my mother's.
Many had bosoms. A few had breasts
like sweets in twists of coloured paper
or set in frills like chocolates in a box
without the card to show the raspberry cream.
We had to leave the floor bent double.

My best partner cleared the glitterball by inches,
squares of light swimming her shoulders.
I'd seen her long grave face in a book of mosaics.
She was the Empress Theodora
but told me her name was Penny.
How everyone said That's lucky
or That's why you keep turning up.
I thought up lots of penny jokes,
but never told anyone. They were too serious.
I wanted to tell them to Penny one day.
She had a tin of raspberry cachous

and let me lean my head on her long lean chest.
I imagined she had breasts.
I imagined her imagining she had.

When I go to the library tomorrow
the titles on all the spines will flare
and I'll take down a book on ballroom dancing.
The Waltz is first, feet lead off the page
and ribs of print will read the hunger of my hands.
'Penny,' I'll say, 'I went to Ravenna
and saw the Empress Theodora.
She shares your eyes, your mouth, your pallor.'
I'll press each page against my cheek,
then close it, weigh dancing in my hands,
and slide it back in three-four time
in 793.33.

FAR AWAY SOUNDS STRANGE

Behind a broken fence, tickets pinned in
her hair, a woman in green dressing gown
sits on her step, rolls a cigarette, inhales
and clasps her breasts as if she might have won.
She'd be the same age now. Would I know her?

MB lets you do her lets . . . *the graffiti*
stop as though they'd forgotten what they'd started
to say. A shock of lust. I turn away.
Was it Mary perhaps? The kids are smashing
part of a machine I can't identify.

Maureen or Molly? It won't come. The kids'
noise, a dog's howling and the roar of planes
and in between – silences, no sounds of
birds – all fixed in glass, a paperweight
I could shift at any time, for instance

Now. I play a bass note and through it soars
a woman's voice and I, not we not yet,
start over. The smells. Yes, they're more difficult.
What the frayed blue curtains, the colourless
carpet, the walls themselves have each absorbed.

Out of the brown door that might have been hers
a kitchen smell and, close behind, a cloud
of history, a stuffiness so strong
it knocks me back, longing precise and fierce
for a childhood that's mine as well as hers.

I drink the smell I never knew I sought.
The four knots in the rug. Desire's roots run
straight. Let her become you, filling those spaces
in your head, a haunting I know's a fiction.
You, yes. I can only talk to a you.

The woman in green lifts a ticket, *This'll*
be the winner. I nod. She pulls her gown
closer. *D'you wanna come in for a coffee?*
Thank you, but I've got to go. I used to
be a looker, she says. *Still are,* I say.

She could be you, same colour eyes, but no.
The lost address, your forgotten name. No,
I won't look for you. Wherever you are
it won't be here. We never touched. We almost
did. When you said where you were from. This place.

THE RIDING ROOM

Bare boards, curtains of dust all stuck together
and the horse's tail glued in its bottom. The hairs
aren't dead for when we yank at them half-scared
the horse leaps in the air and breaks its tether,
and then kicks back. Dust rises from the rockers
between boards stained like gravy round the skirting.
Smack smack its round grey side. It doesn't hurt it.
Giddyup. Beneath the window is the knocker.

Mysterious callers come to our front door
and there's a Wolseley with an oval light.
Rock gently. Shsh. We rock across the floor
over the heads of Mr and Mrs Brown
who shout and scream when we're awake at night.
Rock rock we both go up we both come down.

HORSES

It's so high that I slip down the dapple grey sides
stretching my legs on the back of his back. Hold on
to the pole, and the man in the middle comes swinging
like he doesn't care, takes my money and I want to say,
Look at my feet on the stirrups, but dad's turned away.

The girl on the bay horse waves Mum! I go up
and a spiral flute screws through my fingers
forcing a silver taste, peeling the glitter off
underneath metal, my dapple grey horse going up
going down and I hang on the rope of his slippery mane.

Long chains of white lights swaying out . . .
and the man in the middle leans to the woman on blue.
She tosses her head and her hair streams out and I see
how it works, where iron goes through a slot in the floor
and overhead cranks pull the silvery poles up and down.

The girl on the bay is calling to me, Are we over water?
I look her Who cares? and she shouts, Are we halfway yet?
like she plays at the seaside and shows me the spiral
red in the palm of her hand. We're in a circle of light.
We're in air over water. We're floating, we're flying.

Let's get off, she says, but it's going too fast and we can't
get off. The woman on blue roan is crying, she's sad,
but the seasidey girl simply laughs as the man in the middle
sits down beside her. She laughs as he comes and he goes
and they're going so fast that I never catch up.

The lights burn brighter, the organ plays louder,
the horses go faster through nights and through days,
the days getting shorter the nights getting colder
till the mothers and fathers get tired of waiting,
then button their coats and lie down on the ground.

When will it end? says the seasidey girl and her hair's
gone grey and my knees have gone stiff
up and down in the stirrups, the lights have burnt out
and the man in the middle will never come back.
The spiral of holding's cut deep in her palm.

She says, Night's coming on and I want to get off.
There's no light in the field and none in the distance
and no one is dancing or waving a torch, nobody yelling
or kicking a beer can. There's nothing at all.
I say, Night's all around, and we get off together.

HARTSTONGUE

Hartstongue woman, how you amaze me
with your beds that need watering
through endless heats, your level eyes,
your knowing of strange plants and places.
The fern you sell me has black bars
beneath its narrow glossy blades.
By its looks it should grow in wet
mossy places, drenched in cloud,
but you say it will grow in a dry wall.
Your even voice. Well you should know.

Hartstongue woman of rare plants, rank weeds,
raised beds, of strong and useful body,
tell me the habits of this fern of yours.
I know why it's called hartstongue, yes,
but tell me again in your even voice.
Soothe me with knowledge, talk of soils
and like the sunflower turn round.
Tell me of your endless watering this summer,
how you cooled your wrists and your hands
under the hose when you finished planting.

Hartstongue woman, show me the dirt
in your nails, your arms washed white.
Tell me how the heat strikes from the earth
this summer, bakes your feet and ankles,
rises up your legs. How each plant needs
your care, breathes in and out with you,
its precious moisture softening the air.
The fern is glossy in your dusty arms.
Let me choose another fern of yours
in the breathlessness of the glasshouse.

Hartstongue woman, moisten your tongue,
talk plants to me, the Latin names,
the common names, all you remember
in the heat of the day. Talk ferns to me
with your level eyes, uncurl your hands
like these soft fronds. Dirt clings to both,
so hot your sweat tracks through the dust,
Deer, hart, why don't you run? I've got
your scent. Like any dog I want to lick
salt from your legs with my slippery tongue.

YOUR GARDEN AT MYALUP, WA

for Elaine and Tony

'I feel as if I've been dragged reluctantly to paradise,' Jackie

I woke the first day to see honeyeaters
and counted nine green parrots in the tree,
the little eucalypt with feathery flowers.
Red over their beaks, and heads as dark as plums,
pale blue undertails – see how well you taught me –

and green so bright they must have stolen it
from the dust-coloured trees, down each wing
one last brushstroke of fluorescent lime.
They cracked the seeds – and then white magpies drove
them off and rang melodious bells like lepers.

Not the way I'd say 28, your name for them,
more like twinyite as if your birds repeat
the Cockney, Scots and Irish in the voices.
Next day pink galahs and kookaburras,
wattle and butcher birds, the blue-tailed wren.

You plant in compost in fine pale sand
that's always blowing and your dune garden grows
kangaroo paw and peppermint tree,
palm and fig, and orange butterflies
with thick black veins while the big gum leans over.

I had no names for things I saw, and when
I did they didn't fit. Your herring isn't mine.
Place names so often left by conquered peoples
and their lost meanings always haunt my tongue
with thoughts of Eden where things first got named.

You have your other ghosts as well. At dusk
the watchful kangaroos, their slender faces
as sensitive as deers'. Such unfamiliar
stars only your neighbour knows the Southern Cross.
And autumn, invisible without the fall.

IN WHICH FLAGS ARE LAID

Tilt the top one, get the weight
and feel, dint the ground, scrawk it
down, angle-roll it to the sand bed.

Anyone that works with stone knows
about the Incas, their walls of multi-
angled blocks, no gap for knives.

Learn to move slowly. This is the
first. It doesn't have to fit with others.
The next butts up, lies snug.

Stone, gentler in the hand than brick.
The third doesn't want to go.
Knock and rub them up against.

Trees and flowers among rocks
in Italian painting. The Palatine,
the *foro romano* in its ruined state.

Spit blots and is absorbed. Powder
smooths fingers, drinks from the hand.
I wrestle flags to walk on fixedness.

One stands proud. Scrape out,
level, twist and tamp, but it rocks
corner to corner, won't find its home.

The City paved with river-bedded
sandstone, iron red ripples in
its grey, grey-blue and yellow ochre.

Sedimentary rock, passivity made
firm. A blade will pass between
in places. Sand under, nudge up. Solid.

THE COURTYARD SWEEPER'S KINDNESS

Our priest has found prints in the bowl of myrrh,
the obsidian gleams less brilliantly in places
and he's busy reckoning what extremes of pain
he can measure to the sacrilegious fur
I hold against my skin beneath my jacket.
I know him well. Red is his favourite stain.

Red rug running down the limestone walkway.
In gaps between the flags there's yellow grain,
melon seeds, feathers, wool clotted with blood.
Keeping out magpies, starlings and the sparrows,
washing the endless floors when there's no rain,
some job. To get it clean we want a flood.

He hasn't seen me. Now the outer court.
Poppies torn from cracks are wilting in the sun.
The neophytes proceed on hands and knees,
their pointed elbows knock their narrow breasts.
They watch for figs, leaves shooting from a drain
and camomile. They weed the stone. No one sees.

He broods behind the black curtain. I'm out
and going down the steps, past the old boy
soling shoes for emperors, past the mufti,
the mage, the rabbi. *They're gone!* he shouts.
I go down through his pastures fenced with bones
to the river where the kittens drown in safety.

A COLD DAY AND I DRINK GREEN TEA BY THE WINDOW

A bamboo handle arcs over the belly of the pot whose brown earth
swims with leaves plucked from hills where winter air
is colder than this cold, the swirl of leaves unfurling
countries and provinces so dry they give up their savour.

Sparrows come and go, brown flakes falling sideways.
Enough air to stir small branches. The clouds move
in a speechless rush. I am sipping green the bushes have lost.
A robin and goldfinches. It is cold. I am sipping green.

Once I pronounced *misled* as *mizzled,* thinking of a mistle thrush.
Misled myself. The Sanskrit *dhyana,* pronounced in Chinese
as *Chan,* then in Japanese as *Zen* becomes less like the leaf
of the spreading fig, the Bodhi tree, and more like tea.

In a shop I saw three iron teapots, one with iron flowers,
one the shape of a flattened gourd and one with two ridges
running round it that I followed with my fingers, learning
their presence and their weight. I followed with my fingers.

Their iron handles moved with a satisfying resistance
against the lugs. I looked for grains of the moulding sand
they were cast in, but found none. I found none.
Repetitions soothing and irritating. Repetitions, grains of sand.

Above the snowdrops, the red cups of japonica.
There are scratches on the white wall, but when I look
they are the opposite of that, marks where something has rubbed
    off
part of itself. Part of itself become part of the wall.

I marvel at Hokusai in his old age. His silent waterfalls, motionless, not moving as they fall so they are falling up as much as down. The water is blank paper among rocks, water defined as absence. I'm falling in a steam of tea.

TO THE DIFFICULT RESOLUTION

Vienna, September 1826

Bang! Out of the soundboard through gaps through felt
fingers strike keys for metal-song,
my hands compelling me the way the old drunk
dragged me out of bed to practice.
Practice? This is the music,
speaking its trial at these hands,
from out of nothing this then this,
sounds I heard before I can remember, when I saw them
sticking to his fingers or flying from the clavichord.
Notes, not startled magpies. The wire answers
the hammer, lifts hairs on my neck. A father
that pitied himself. To learn the old music, own it,
let it go. Get length, pitch, sound!
A cart on the cobbles. *Bang!*
Darkness, but I will throw it out again and again.

I dreamed last night the shepherd played his flute.
A flute cut out of lilac wood
says my friend. Lilac wood!
I listen, watch the shepherd's cheeks fill,
his fingers move . . . and the flute is silent.
Can't you hear?
The heart rushes every barricade
and what spills from the thrush's throat,
the meadow pipits at their trills and peeps,
streams rushing to the Rhine, great shaggy trees
and those that are too bright
resound in exhausted sleep.
From a valley in my dream – *cuckoo! cuckoo!*
Woods and rocks produce the echo man desires to hear.
Gentleness, not that of the wife-beater

sobbing when the beating's done,
but the man who splits stones by day
and by rushlight finds intervals and semi-tones,
keys responding before they're struck.
One hand keeps falling as a leaf falls,
under-playing, almost unnoticed,
the trickle of notes carried along, bearing their own end.

Don't interrupt if I can hear you, and, if I can't,
don't.
Musicians have fixed note length by device,
with no invention. Limitations are what we work with
and against, they say. No!
We work with noises infinitely divisible
or sustained, chords stronger than joy.
But such anger pours from your allegro.
Let me play in my room
or an opera house and anger
thrown back, walls buckling, doors banging, the clapping claque,
Célie, Hélène, Shoshanne . . .
and the gentlest of these,
how should I know but in the apprehension of my heart?

More pedal! Get higher notes, quicker hammers
to make the Rhine flow backwards.
Forte without strength. Erhard, Broadwood –
harps without Vienna's singing, without its touch or action.
None of them sounds.
More volume! Higher deeper notes!
Make a machine I can rise on to an over-heaven.
hammer makers, wire drawers.
Not limits, not black and white, not eternal brightness,
but the world itself, my blues and greens . . .
and my darling red, the puissant horse
I ride the mysterious barriers through.

To be among the great and realise one's inferiority.
Names are limitations, descriptions of plumage, call and flight.
A second Mozart,
but these are no harpist's hands, not Mozart's
with his fine choppy playing, for he had no legato.
Tinky tink tinky tink. None.
From Haydn I learned nothing. Yet Handel
makes music from a handful of notes
the way sunlight cuts leaf against leaf,
leaves making a tree, trees a forest.
What is it to be known?
I play to Goethe and he weeps.
This is not applause, I want the sound of hands.
And my Berlin audience so educated
so refined all they can do is stagger towards me
with emotion, a thing irrelevant to me
the crude enthusiast, Ludwig the vulgar.

I walk and the air is soft, thoughts streaming
with cross winds with precise complexities.
Rewrite towards perfection. Too difficult?
What is difficult is good and beautiful.
A galloping horse! All nature is an inspiration.
Sing, yell, stamp until the ground returns
slow and strong like thunder. For the Holy Spirit
bird calls on the flute and on the Kyrie I wrote
From the heart – may it return to the heart.
Endless as deep immeasurable nature
the simplest theme reshapes itself
through every pattern of the heart to one containing all.

Young know-all virtuosos race up the keyboard
while I cough blood. Work, Ludwig! Work!
By a path of his own discovery
he reached that height of excellence on which he stands.

Remembered praise soothes me
and I look across green plains to mountains
at the end of sight where more and more I want to be.
My pianos are out of tune, they say.
If strings keep breaking, make stronger strings!
I always strike too hard, kneeling on these boards
to feel the music. My bones connect
and the instrument needs me the way every instrument
needs – with its whole frame.
I've cut its legs off and we're wrecked.

Legato, second note rising out of the first.
The pedal releases the singing tone.
Notes are not a handful of bright pebbles. They're shapes
and lengths, slates and the nails through slates,
an avalanche, its first reports, each particle
of the world settling, dust gathering around me,
dust on black keys.
I seek the place not-home where I'd return
if roots ran through the father to his father, kapellmeister,
true musician, if leaves floated back
to their appointed places on the branch,
singing when they're struck, their dazed faces.

My visitor writes his question in the book,
glances at the piss pot under the piano, and goes.
Days blink, signalling something I can't make out.
Reading holds back the darkness. *But now Fate catches me.*
Let me not die without a struggle,
without glory, but when I've achieved some great thing
those not yet born shall hear of.
Notes start with an explosion then diminish.
Played backwards, they'd come out of the future
and burst into silence. That's how I'll learn to be, going far ahead,
always returning to lead men onward.

Rondo and ritornello. I always knew how to begin,
but to end where there is no end is against nature.
My scores are published, my staves will unroll
into the future through keyboards more powerful than this
and what is uncreated will be lost.
The last time I conducted they turned me round
to see hands opening and closing like butterflies,
and then I knew they were applauding.
I will to go back to the old music, look its makers
in the eye, and we will play together.

Every key has its character. C minor's anguish,
E major a starry sky. Each one speaks
to a different part of the soul. Once
I would tread the progress of the chords into the land,
C major through the forest, C minor in the fields,
D major as I crossed the Danube,
E flat when I climbed the hills.
Along the streets I read the movement of a theme.
Not in this scrawl across the paper. No,
not crows picking along the wintry furrows,
they do not do. The quill won't hold the ink.

From home I could see the Rhine one side,
on the other the Seven Mountains that looked so near
I wondered if that joyful feeling came from the mountains
or from me. Now I am here
like a shipwrecked sailor and while I am in the world
I want to drink wine with the old farts.
I'll pay for the wine. I didn't mean to be angry.
Such good times. Now I must always be facing south.
At dawn at dusk sun on the Alps. September,
no breeze through the leaves, and then no leaves.

Both pedals, half-pedal, all kinds of staccato,
to the top of the scale and fall. Note
played after note must fade or I'd be a tuning fork
broken. As long as I can keep awake I will
extemporise. A cart on the cobbles. *Bang!*
It had seemed impossible to leave this world
until I'd made all I felt within me.
The work for fiddles needs an ending,
the difficult resolution, and when I've finished
I have never finished. Sounds moving forward
for others to repeat.
I hold down the sustain pedal, seek
its interior singing, its uncanniness transcending
hard hammers, cold metal strings.

A GOOD TIME FOR SEA-LIFE

Framed by pictures of whales, sharks,
the varieties of jellyfish, she sits in her hut.
What's the best time for sea-life? I ask.
After a spell of fine weather, she says,
and we might get a plankton bloom,
and it has to be calm and a high cloud,
no shine so nothing reflects but your face.
If you want something different,
if you don't know what you're after,
night is a good time. The boat leaves at ten.

Me and the others, clothes heavy with sand,
give her our tickets and we pitch
through a tunnel of powerful light, past seals,
and past jellyfish she nets up to show us.
Then we stop, For the dolphins, she says,
and by the way my name's Kate and this
is a good night, smooth water, and dolphins
are here. And they are. Or they're rocks.
When she peels off and dives she makes
no reflection. She calls Why don't you join me?

I do. It's so cold in the sea's gleaming black
there's no time to think between yelling
as if I see a glass dropped, a table walked into.
What I see is a creature, a woman, a fish,
markings of phosphor, a swerving of thoughts,
a ribby thing saying Ooh, Isn't it lovely.
Next day I long for the sound of her pleasure,
the water she swims through. I say, Kate!
She says, If you know what you're after
night is a good time. The boat leaves at ten.

The sun once on the water,
        once on the sand under it.
The fish are a distraction,
        they and their writing
on the rippling bed seen
        through a gentle swell.
So we'll let the fish go,
        reluctantly, and floating pebbles
of white pumice that might be
        sea-worn polystyrene
except they do not ride so high.
        And we'll let the underwater sun
on underwater sand go too.
        Hard to tell which hollows
of the sea the gleams come through
        before its hills move on,
half carrying half letting slip
        a coil of diesel from the harbour.
Let surface be enough,
        rings of light along the rim
of each caldera, ductile gold
        drawn out until one O becomes
two so there's the flash
        of an 8 lassoing nothing
and that's the bait. Where air
        touches sea the metal cry
of sun snakes circling. A broken O's
        a hook – from which come
lover and love's object –
        but on the sea no O is broken
unless it's joined again. That
        is its courtesy. Let me practise.
O O. It's not so hard. Round out
        the lips. O your brilliants,
your fingers at the silk edge . . .

WINTER AT THE SEASIDE CAFÉ

It's still here. It never shuts. Steam shushes
into milk as buzzlights chase themselves
on the fruit machine. It's not warm,
but we're out of the breeze that's pushing sand back
to the beach. The pipe and beard, he was here last time
or someone very like him. Those two, black jeans,
green lycra skirt, two pairs of boots, are tired
from wanting as though they've spent too long swimming
towards each other and now she's sweating
in the cold café. Passion or drugs or both,
it's hard to say. Those who can't sleep, looking
for the words, no place to go but here.

Back then we gazed through this same glass,
still green with salt, at people passing,
strange names in the marine aquarium
and guessed which was a John, a Jane or Sue
as we clasped each other's knees or you checked
my eyes flicking between your eyes, legs, breasts.
We touch hands lightly now. A gull's wings folded.

The criss-cross pattern brown formica hasn't changed,
cigarette burns, edges chipped, but clean.
It's been so polished that it's worn to white in places,
a heaven behind the dark net of design.
We look out, imagine looking in.
The café's a lantern shifting in the wind
and the dawn is a rumour on the sea-roads.
Another hour, the colours will surface,
seek something to stick to, drift down the parterre
to the tin tables and settle on the chairs
as if the music's stopped. Did we notice then?
Your body was flickering with light.

He's got the earring, she has the green hair.
Don't go, she says, *I want to stay with you.*
This is the passage from the old story.
The mermaid's on dry land. That's why she sweats.
Remember last time we were here? you say
and try to catch the lamplight in your fingers
as if it were warm sand trickling through.

HOW THE WRONG THOUGHT GREW

It wasn't that the tree was leaning. All the trees
were leaning in the wind off that sea, the wind
that was always more or less. When it was less
my companions started talking but no one
got out more than two words together, though
in their heads they practised making speeches,
their eyes watering with the pressure of thought.

Something was wrong with the angle of the branches
and the undersides of the leaves were too visible.
What then made me move towards it? To discover
the fantastic shapes ignorance takes in the mind?
I knew it would be better if I didn't know. I knew
once I touched the pale down of the leaves all
would change and I'd become the others' mark.

ABOVE WATER

They bring me their disasters.
When I ask why a job
has not been done
has not been done well
there is usually a disaster behind it.

Sometimes they tell me the length and breadth of it
how many people were drowned
why they didn't see the iceberg
and I listen.
They rarely say they're the ones that are drowning.
So I say When you are drowning hold on to your work.
It is your lifebelt. It is a firm thing in your life.

Then we discuss how the task that seems impossible
can be done piece by piece
like a pile of ironing.
We talk about all the obvious things
how to start
how to continue
how to ask for help
and we agree a timetable.

Then I say Let's talk briefly of matters of the heart,
and I see their eyes widen slightly
as if a heart were
a thing you kept at home
a dog you left tied up outside the office door.

I say Leave your despair at home
whatever's left of your home,
but find your anger and bring it me.
This work needs your anger and you will do it well.
They look at me and go.

When I shut the door, the sea floods in.
The sea roars in my ears.

FROM THE *HISTORIA GALACTICA*

(Humans in their 21st Century)

You may have heard how their pilots were all blind,
tapped the passing stars with the tips of their white eyes
and used a forgotten drug to navigate the spaceways
of what we call time-and-time-again, how they reported
seing the luminous nets stretch and bend around them,
a ball dress in a blizzard, bare head and shoulders
bearing on a field of prime snow, deep and unconsolidated,
they wore as mantle of their dedication, their power.
While none of this is true exactly, they never learned to fly
by feeling or understand lives other than their own.

They made many journeys to friends or relatives
(we discussed these concepts), but mostly on commerce
and were skilled in moving between situations,
their plays so nuanced the air was stillstill.
Put yourselves in their silences. The voice of their trainer,
calm, patient, in control, as they had to be, and when
their concentration failed, the childhood voices of carers
and enemies. Consider what led them to the heights
they occupied. Do not believe they were mooncold.
Understand how light more than darkness distorts perception.

They experienced the world as desperate attraction
to photon sources, what we call the blue nightflowers,
the way they flashed decisions from a glance
like a spinning coin, while they lippylipped the reverse.
Imagine for a moment how they processed fingertips,
sweetpoints, needlekisses coming at them quicker
than they could reel them in, resolving the swift take
of detail, turbulence factored out. Remember
they were muscle tied on bone. The risk that jagged them
was others coming too close, and then not close enough.

THE SIDE ROOM

South of the river and desperate for a drink
I find this road house between brick estates.
The bar is full. I open a side door
on a quiet room where curtains are drawn

but let grey light through rents and holes, enough
for me to see five men in jackets, no ties,
round a table in a stupor. The bar is free.
'If you stay in here you best be quiet,'

the barmaid says 'then they won't notice you,
the boys.' I drink, and suddenly
like mechanical chimes they jerk to life.
'Let's get shivved up,' says one, and pulls his knife.

He stabs the air, stands up and makes new holes
in the curtains, expelling words like solids
from his muscled mouth. 'Here's to the don of dons,'
they cry and knife the air. One lays a doll

on the table top and says 'Let's get the bastard,'
stabbing its chest. The others do the same.
'Cut off the arms and legs. Leave it with stumps.'
I start as they turn to stare, not at, but through me.

They don't see anyone except themselves.
They say 'We have no knowledge of this murder,
we were not involved, we did not kill . . .'
Then one stands up scanning an unseen crowd.

'What're you staring at? Come on. I'll take you,'
and returns to the stupor I found when I came in.
The barmaid clears the mess and fills their glasses.
I ask 'How often does this happen?'

'All afternoon, all evening, every day
since the killing,' she says. 'I hang new curtains
every day. I change the table cover
every week.' 'Who pays for it?' I ask.

'One of their fathers, known around these parts.'
'Don't you feel sorry for them?' I say.
'To tell the truth', she says, 'I wish them dead.'
They wake, and stab the air again, and curse.

THE CARPETMAKERS

Waterlight flows and loops across the ceiling
playing keys too high or low to hear
except for us brought up to treadling
on the floor of the room beside the river.

Although we cannot rise we feel the notes
rise through us bone by bone jumping the joints
to reach our fingers plying instead of playing.
Our eyes are the only things we own.

We're told to keep them on the work, their work,
the bright blue light blue threads of wool
that pull like paddled water, but our eyes
turn sideways glide to where waves turn

like bodies which are not ours and never
could be, and longly loosely stretch their sunlines,
moonlimbs, green veins of waterweed.
In shade we have to learn each shade of blue.

We see our bodies being worked till light
refuses to reflect from us we're so invisible
so that our knees age, swell and seize.
We know, even if we weren't treadling

this floor, they'd never let us paddle through
those watched but unimaginable waters
that flicker on the ceiling, as far from us
as we are from being held by our dead mothers.

To supply its people the city had a cistern
cut in the rock, its water huge and blue,
square like solid truth they saw right through
and so believed that no such thing existed.

DECEMBER FIELD

Steel shine on clay prepared for absence,
air moving over ridges, clods and flints
between hedges and fences, under frosts.
Its nakedness. A length and breadth
not limitless, but reckonable measures.

More than the copse with rooks' nests
in its rigging and its last few leaves,
this bareness pulls some longing out of me,
a thread that runs and cannot find its end.
The unguarded gaze is my worst betrayer.

Nothing protects it. Furrows are tremors
from some new disturbance, steam rising
from the broken soil. The share's cut and turn
turns towards the ending of another year
the passion in the straightness of its lines.

The weeds are gone except their seed,
land cleared of all that was attached.
If to finish well is letting go, December earth,
its intense withdrawal and pull to ground,
understands how I might choose to leave.

DOWN ADDINGFORD STEPS

Before Morrison's car park it was Farrand's Yard
the way I came that summer through the ginnell
between the Kayes and Mrs Audsley's house,
a sandstone tunnel strange winds had blown
to let the light in and the Yarders out.
Above the arch a window, always shadowed,
held a small vase. No face was ever there,
no eyes, but in the vase pipe cleaners, spills,
yellowed newspaper torn to look like flowers.
The sun climbed halfway to my belt, then I
was out by Mr Gooder's door just where
my mother always paid the rent, the smiles
of wanting to be thought good tenants, notes
carefully folded, the book signed and closed.

Fast past the Peel Street doors and up to Shepstye
where I let Kim loose and he went mad
as if he'd never smelt a hayfield, nosing
black stinks and pissingposts. I put my fingers
into stones of the wall, each one licked out
like butter, its yellow sand seeking the seas
that laid it down, the net of resistant mortar
protruding, so it glued together no more
than the idea of its builder, only its capstones
intact, a ghost wall catching air and cobwebs,
the spiders watching me through bright bead curtains
as Mrs Audsley watched us in the yard.

We tumbled through a gap to the valley's lip
into a minted morning, and only air between.
Addingford Steps go down a tumbling cliff,
ochre and rust-red sandstone blocks, part carved
to level treads, a concrete step in places,

one zig-zag with an iron handrail drilled
and cemented in the rock, the staining of rust
reddening the rock's own red, and halfway down
a clump of tansy. The yellow buttons my mother
loved for their harsh scent, I loved because she did,
the way she put her nose in them and breathed
as though a saint had stopped and blessed them.

Once down, a red brick bridge across the cutting,
past which lines branch and fill the flat,
dull rails with rusty rolling stock, fern-like,
prints in a block of shale a miner showed me.
I would have gone past the groaning coal-loader
to the shunting yard and listened to the wagons,
as faint and fainter couplings joined their music
to an horizon where I felt that sadness
cover the hills, painfully sweet and strong,
calling, always calling me against my will –
but a train came, and the dense smoke was a heaven
in which the bridge, my feet, everything was lost,
the intense smell of coal and its nimbus of light,
my idea of what the Holy Ghost might be,
its insubstantial substance leaving flecks
of soot in my hair in case I doubted it.

Through spikes of rosebay busy peeling seed
for summer snow, I sauntered through the slow
seductive drift, down river to The Fleet,
a knot of dark brick houses round a mill.
A tarmac road slicked through the fields and stopped.
I knocked and Derek's sister Katherine
opened the door, pink towel round her hair,
a curler sticking out, pink slippers,
blue dressing gown. 'Our Derek's gone to play
with Colin.' Her neck began beneath her gown

and went all the way to her ears and when
she spoke I saw her throat move like a mouse
under a handkerchief. A clean white one.
'What are you staring at?' She slammed the door.

I found myself a stick and one for Kim
and stood beheading flowers by the verge,
whatever raised its head above the rest.
I didn't like Colin. He knew about cocks
and balls and all the proper names for things
and how you could get babies with your spunk
and when I said spunk wasn't that, it meant
having courage, he stood and laughed at me.
He knew I had no courage since he'd seen
me run away when they were hitting Luke.

I turned to see oak leaves grow on a willow,
and on its lower branches clumps of brown hair
hung out to dry like Mary's hair, forlorn
against her grubby neck as she sat on
her doorstep in the sun holding an apple.
The trees were decked with hair and dirty rags
as if no more was left of all the Marys
in the world. Mum said I couldn't go inside
her house and so the day Mary got me
an apple, I waited on the steps uncertain
whether she was girl or woman, her voice
so far away and soft, the way she dressed
like a princess in clothes she never washed
and wore to rags. I looked deep in the willows
fearing to see lodged in a twisting fork
a face, a limb, a hand offering an apple,
but saw the hair was dead grass, the oak leaves
grew on their own oak branch left in the willow
by the thing that left the rags, dead grass, the pools

of mud and combed the hayfield all one way,
brylcreemed it flat with stinking ooze, then sank.
The end house at The Fleet had a sign to say
how the river came through the bedroom once.

I brought the courage I hadn't got, my yellow
I wouldn't give a name, down to the river
to mix my shame with its dull dirty water
and minimise mine with 'for after all
I'm not so bad.' For 'after all' excuses
all before it starts to speak, sweeps up
the mess and lets it go, past here, past now.
I never saw bright water on that stream,
its only bubbles methane from the mud,
detergent suds we used to poke with sticks
or watch them flying on a windy day.
I watched it go, fast flow, though nothing broke
the surface, slight changes in my dull reflection
among upwellings blacker than the rest,
a mass in motion toiling with itself,
on its long slide to sea, the final sewer.

I ran to the echo bridge up iron steps
into the covered footbridge by the railway,
pitch black except through gaps in planks
where shadows of bolted girders surfed the water,
and forced myself to wait half way for the rumbling.
Steps on the stairs and someone coming. Now.
Where its head should be a single brilliance
flashed. 'Hey up. Whaddya doing, lad?'
His face was black, his lips and eyes were pink,
a helmet on his head, his light switched on.
'Waiting for a train.' He laughed and I ran off
to the reedy pond I'd netted daphnia from,
along with cyclops, mayfly larvae, glassworms

to feed the swordtails, angel, and black molly.
I loved to watch the invisible glassworms swim,
except for eyes, nothing but pure refraction,
as real angels would be, dressed in the air
out of our mouths, if we had eyes to see.
With no net, no jam jar, I ate my apple,
people and family out of sight, above,
on high, where St Peter's bells beat the air
and never reached where the deep silence pooled
around my apple, Kim splashing in the pond
by the canal, between the valley sides
where in the cutting trains passed by unheard.

I flicked the fireman's helmet. Pods exploded,
firing their black seeds, detonating more,
my model of atomic fission, Dad's
passion for science fiction, American mags.
I touched the pointed ends with fingertips,
felt them fire into my palm, disgust and pleasure.
Seed pods like jewel earrings on fine wires,
exotic pinky flowers offering cups
that looked as if they might hold poisoned wine
which I would drink then grow like them, my feet
in fetid ditchwater, my skin turned livid,
blotched with purple like Katherine with the rash
she covered up with calomine, and jewels
around my neck, in both my ears, on all
my fingers, my lips wide open and pink forever
and my mother would be ashamed of me
and what my father would say I didn't know
except 'Your mother'd be ashamed of you.'
She wouldn't like it if I called on Derek
because his mum would have to give me dinner.

'Can Derek come out to play?' 'Come in.'
Derek was eating bread and jam at table
opposite his dad's pie and potatoes.
'Don't they have any bate at your house, lad?'
said his dad, getting up to go back to work. His mum
made us hot custard pudding. Katherine sulked.

Then we were gone, Kim barking as we ran.
'Katherine's cross because she's got a rash,'
says Derek, 'and can't go swimming and swank
in that new costume she's got that shows her tits.'
Facing across a field the deserted mill
rode the green furrows. With its truncated chimney,
stone sides, blank windows it was the *Lusitania*,
before the Germans sent her to the bottom,
mid-ocean in the picture book I had.
Nearby, sentinel over waving grass,
the graceful curve of a broken gas lamp.
I pictured mill girls walking across the sea,
the lamp their only star in a stormy night,
shouting, laughing, singing in their head scarves
as I'd seen them at The Fleet after their shift.
The upper floor was gone and where slates slipped
nine diamonds of sky shafted the gloom.
Under iron pillars, overhead mainshaft,
rotting boards, the frightening flutter of birds
we found a magazine of women half
undressed, sitting on swings, standing in fields,
smiling on every page their secret smiles.
They were not real. They didn't work and sing.

We went exploring over Bulcliffe way
then Derek had to go and get his tea.
Across the valley I saw against the sky
a place I didn't know, a fairy village

silhouetted, whose lights came on in ones
and twos, like in a colouring book I had,
where people wore bright velvet cloaks as smooth
as Mary's special dress she let me touch,
and when they talked like people telling stories
their words lit different colours in the air
that made me laugh and cry despite myself.
I looked and laughed to see their tiny church's
columned steeple just like St Peter's, then faintly
with a shock I heard its bells. The breaking sound
shook me as I imagined the flooding river
broke its black waters in the clouded night
and took the Fleeters in their floating beds –
for it was St Peter's, the fairy village
was the town. It had been watching all along.

Over canal, river, railway, one last time
I stopped on steps now losing heat and called
to Kim, then kneeled to touch those slabs of rock
half in hope and half in fear to feel
their elephant rhythm, their breathing through.
I'd read of things 'cut in the living rock'
and wondered what sort of men dared drill
this flesh, split and quarry it, whether they feared,
like butchers, to see slabs jumping off the blocks
and cry to be united with the main.
That summer I felt my old belief grow tender,
wanting to protect it from what I learned at school,
knowledge I'd been getting, a line of wedges,
and knew I couldn't make myself believe
much longer because the world would chivvy me
like an oyster waiting to be opened, its meat
cut out after the knife point seeks an in.
So I stroked the iron-stained rock, its hard rind,
then swept the strip of light above the hills

that called to me 'Come over the world's edge
towards a longing not even you imagine,
a radiance so sweet and strong it hurts'
and watched that tender glow fade out and leave
the bare land lonelier, crying for comfort
in the night to come, and felt my heart go out.